TRANSLATIONS AND POEMS

Andy Gaus

TRANSLATIONS
AND POEMS

Andy Gaus

ANSERINE BOOKS

"The Fox and the Farmer" and "The Humorist" appeared in *Max and Moritz and Other Bad Boy Stories & Tricks,* ©2003 James A. Rock & Co. Publishers. Used by permission.

"Requiem for a Woman," "Lament," "Pont du Carrousel," "Evening," "from Songs of Young Girls," "Lovesong," "The Loneliness," "The Flamingos," "The Gazelle," "The Panther," "The Last Supper," and "Autumn Day" appeared in *Requiem for a Woman and Selected Lyric Poems,* Threshold Books, 1981, and some selections also appeared earlier in the Wesleyan University *Cardinal* and the *Adlit* of Middletown Alpha Delta Phi.

"The Roman Fountain at Borghese," "Meditation," and "Come to the Park They Left for Dead" appeared in the *North Dakota Quarterly.*

"Autumn Day" and "Sonnet to Orpheus #9" appeared in *Rilke Reconsidered,* ed. Sigrid Bauschinger and Susan L. Cocalis, Francke Verlag, 1995.

Thanks to my poetry gang at Wesleyan—

Michael Wolfe, Kabir Edmund Helminski, and Richard Wilbur

FOREWORD

Vesle Fenstermaker was a poet and a family friend as I was growing up in Indianapolis. After her death her writer friends put out a memorial volume of her poetry (*Depth of Field*, Writers Center of Indianapolis, 1996). It's a fine book, and I'm pleased to own a copy.

As I looked at it, I found myself asking whether anybody would do the same for me. And then I asked why anybody else should have to, and why I should demurely wait till after my death to see whether it gets done or not, when I can do the job better and more easily myself now.

It's not a large job. Most of what I have is early work; in later years my energies have mostly gone over to songwriting. There's enough to make one book. There won't be a Volume II.

I'm calling the book *Translations and Poems* because translations make up more than half of it and because the translations, on the whole, outclass the originals. My imitation Rilke is more of a poet than I am.

I don't imagine that this volume will circulate very far. It doesn't have to. With single-copy printing on demand, it's not necessary to have a thousand copies printed, keep 996 of them in storage forever, and take a huge loss. Instead, the copies will be few but placed in appropriate homes, and I hope to make dozens of dollars.

Andy Gaus
Boston, May 2014

CONTENTS

TRANSLATIONS AND POEMS

INSTRUCTIONS

Oh let my poems move as in first gear
And never rush nor speed, and stop but never stall.
Let the first line gently push and feed
The motor starting. Let the last line fall
As dying motors fall. Let it be a poem
Like an old car on a cold day
That was never out of danger but got you safely home.

DRIVING WEST

the sun lights down on the hood for us
at the end of every westward-driving day:
the fourth such sun will find us there

I have looked at my first tumbleweed,
seen desert soil, and the hide-and-seek of mesas,
and rediscovered
truths not known since childhood:

that the sky is a blue mixing-bowl inverted
that the clouds hang there by magic and do not fall
that the stars of night are not three, nor twelve, but myriad
that the sky enclosing these is black

I have gained this much: that I saw New Mexico blue
and the land still bright with flamecolor—vistas
that spun and bounced off mountainsides to the valleys
                                        below them—
as, counting myself twenty-three years old and soon
                          twenty-four,
I crossed through Texas real
and Oklahoma physical
to the certainty of California
my first West, and the world's last

THE CONE

"Oh! I'm so sorry!" But SPLAT went the cone on the ground.
I fried in my shame.
                         He took no offense.
He was black. He shrugged, and smiled, and was off.
He probably made a full and complete recovery.
I never did. I've been embarrassed for the rest of my life.
In heaven I get to buy that man an ice-cream cone.

RAINER MARIA RILKE:
THE ROMAN FOUNTAIN AT BORGHESE

Two basins, one the other half concealing,
Rising from old and rounded marble bands,
And from the topmost water gently kneeling
To meet the lower water where it stands,

Hearing its soft words dumbly, and revealing,
In secrecy, as if from hollow hands,
Behind the green and darkness, heaven's ceiling,
Like some as yet unnoticed circumstance;

Itself at peace, and in the lovely basin
Spreading without nostalgia, loops from loops,
Where now and then, and dreamingly, the drops

Lower themselves along the mossy trimmings
To the last looking-glass, whose basin sleeps
And smiles from underneath with overbrimmings.

THE WINDOWS OF YOUR SOUL...

The windows of your soul, the eyes, are glass
That lets the light, but not the image, pass.
We only know that if we wait a while
Your smile hops up, and quickly smiles.
It never breaks the window and escapes,
But presses close enough to scrape
The glass—at which we startle and look round,
Trying to guess the substance from the sound,
Trying to think the shadow into shape.

SPEAKING OF HIM

Speaking of him, your eyes illumine your features
Better than candles, framelights under portraits,
Or ever a sly photographer with bulbs.

Speaking of him, your timbre hazes and husks,
Deepens and dusks; but if a clause grew faint,
I would not think of asking you what words.

I cannot fix the reason why a horn
Should make a horse into a unicorn,
Nor yet can I discover
Why I must now regard you with surprise,
As if a cameo could move its eyes
And speak of its lover.

ON A PHOTOGRAPH

It goes to the heart. It couldn't have happened again.
And it's all there.

The beard is part of it, and the full gaze,
But speak any further and I realize
What would have been lost in speaking,
And only was preserved because

Some way, some way or other,
In a random yard, in an off season,
This one-time flower,
This transcendental still, recalled to paper
What each of us in his room alone will see:

You as you might have been;
You as, in spite of everything, you are.

STEFAN GEORGE:
COME TO THE PARK THEY LEFT FOR DEAD

Come to the park they left for dead, and look:
The shimmer of the distant smiling beaches,
Bright clouds, and the unhoped-for blue that reaches
Above the flowered pathways and the brooks.

Come take the tender silver and deep gold
From birch tree and from beech. It is not cold.
A few late roses have not withered yet.
Take them, and as you wind the coronet,

Take too these asters, blooming at year's bottom,
The purple round the tendrils of wild vine.
And what remained of living green, entwine
Delicately around the face of autumn.

SONG:
GLEANINGS

Come with me to the park they left for dead;
See how the green has taken darkness in,
How leaves adorn the land like precious stones
On wrinkled skin.

Treetops no longer melt into the sky,
But speak of trifles in the tender wind;
Bushes that sprang apart and cried aloud
Shut fast again.

Pull out the strands of green among the brown,
The rose whose petals clung when others fell;
Store up your memories while the light recedes,
And hold them still.

THERAPY

We all knew John, his talent and his troubled mind.
We knew he was in great pain and seeing a shrink.
He used to tell us sometimes what his shrink told him:
That we are not actors but victims, all of us,
Victims of each other, victims of circumstance;
And what we call love is no more than two selfishnesses
Striking a temporary bargain.
That's what his shrink said, and he must have believed him,
Cause he jumped out the window of the Howard Johnson's
Twenty-three stories down to the roof of the bar next door.
I've often wondered if I could have talked with him…
I'm sure a lot of us have.
I know what I would have liked to say:
That love, at least sometimes, is delightfully better than that,
And the will is urgently more real.

RAINER MARIA RILKE:
From "SONGS OF YOUNG GIRLS"

Young girls sing:
The time of which our mothers told,
It never reached inside the fold
Where we lay sleeping, smooth and clear.
They say to us that they were felled
By thunderstorms, one stormy year.

What is a storm? We cannot say.

Deep in our tower tucked away
We have to listen from afar
To hear the forest sigh.
One night there was a strange star
That passed by.

And in the garden where we sing,
We tremble, feeling it begin;
Each day we are on guard—

But nowhere is there any wind
To bend us hard.

VALEDICTIONS FOR TWO FRIENDS

I.

I cannot bring myself to say,
Be less passionate or kind,
Clap a padlock on your mind,
Leave no fiber-end exposed,
Keep the door of feeling closed;
Either learn the ways of men,
Or you'll just be hurt again.

For what we need is what you are,
Something desperately rare,
Something needed by the world,
As a climber needs a hold:
Strength, to choose yourself a task
That we could not justly ask.

I only hope you see your mind,
Feel the strength that drives you on,
Hear the impulse from within;
And with that much understood,
I call it good.

II.

You're a big-hearted guy, you're a hirsute rose;
What's gonna happen to you, no one knows—but
This night's the night: don't look out for trouble;
Just dance, throw your weight around the room, talk French,
And smile
          white teeth and black stubble.

THE HIGH ROAD AND THE LOW ROAD

Hauling the Mistress Logic's cart,
Scrambling on with never a stop,
Checking at every step the chart
To fold it immaculately up,
I start to doubt, till I cannot keep
My eyes on the road, I cannot help
But squint, from a corner of eye, just a squint at the sky.

And what do I see but you, aloft like an angel.

I look for your jets, or props; and so does the woman
                                    behind me.
Those curves, I feel how you turn them; I am abashed.
You smile on me as you see me,
And sing to me as you climb:
"Above the clouds there are no more clouds;
Blue, nothing else but blue,"
Through which your course designs itself in real time.

RAINER MARIA RILKE:
AUTUMN DAY

Lord: it is time. The summer has been large.
Lay down across the sundialface thy shadow,
And on the meadow set the winds at large.

Command the fruit be heavy on the vine;
Give them two southern-winded days of leisure;
Propel them to complete themselves; and pressure
The final sweetness in the heavy wine.

Whoever has no house now, goes without.
Whoever lacks a friend, will long be lacking,
Will spend his time in writing, reading, waking,
And through the tree-lined avenues in and out
Restlessly wandering, when the leaves are flaking.

SONG:
LET THE HARVEST TIME BE NEAR

I remember in the springtime
I used to sneak downstairs and run outside.
I blew my questions up like pink balloons
And watched them floating in the deep blue sky.
I had enough to do with playing
In that sweet season of the year.
But now my hands are full of praying:
Let the harvest time be near.

So let the harvest time be fast approaching.
Just leave a few more days of easy time,
To put the fullness in the corn and barley,
To put the sweetness in the wine.
After a springtime full of perfect leisure,
After a summer full of lovely weather,
I want to see it all brought together:
Let the harvest time be near.

I remember in the summer
I lost my bearings in the woods somewhere.
I breathed my secrets in the forest air
In that sweet season of the year.
But now I want to see the crops I've sown,
I want to see them standing fully grown,
And if I may I'd like to bring some home.
Let the harvest time be near.

So let the harvest time be fast approaching.
Just leave a few more days of easy time,
To put the fullness in the corn and barley,
To put the sweetness in the wine.
After a springtime full of perfect leisure,
After a summer full of lovely weather,
I want to see it all brought together:
Let the harvest time be near.

A GIRL AND HER CITY

A clarinet calling up four narrow flights of stairs, or up
To a black-frame window through the neon rain;
Riffing and mordanting out, blasting the range of your range,
Snake out from nowhere, leave no clue when you fade.

Sighting along West Michigan,
Pawnshops and makeshift churches,
The eternal note still ringing in the underside of the ear,
Perspective,
The straits of the eye,
And all compressed into darkness.

That night:
Your face, that I had never seen before with tears,
Your white sweater, heaving, unable to throw off its weight.
When we got in the car,

I turned the tuning knob from end to end:
Stations wavered and went, out of nowhere
A word, a note of a song,
And the long drive home.

*　*　*

On Easy Street, my home, the dogs
And cats will hush when curfew falls,
Beneath a shard of moon concealed
At times behind a single branch.
The slides that are stacked inside my mind
Flash on the ceiling over and over.
Thinking about you, the sounds of sleep
Drone light down Meridian, pass me by.

RAINER MARIA RILKE:
LAMENT

How everything is far
and lost and gone.
I think the star
whose brightness I welcome in
has been extinct for an age.
I think, in the barge
that passed, a voice was afraid.
Back in the house a clock
went dead…
But in what house?…
If I could only get out
of my heart and under the wide sky.
If I could pray.
Surely of all the stars, one
must still be there.
I think I'd know
which one alone
has lasted through; which one
at the beam's end in heaven stands like a silver town.

THE PIANO PLAYER

No more talking. He hits the keys   big chords;
Bickering riffs, tightening trills, grace notes abruptly;
Galloping over the keys. His hands come down like hooves;
He pounds the keys, he pummels them like a son of a bitch.
Big chords again. He's good.

He plays so loud he can't hear himself think.
He narrows his eyes, though he has to look at the keys.
If he could sing his heart out,
He'd sing it across the room and out the door.
How close to obliteration? Not enough.
But that's why he entered the room,
That's why he sat down to play.
And that is what, though he stops and starts and stops again,
That is what, though his words would lead you aside from
                                        the point,
That   is what he is seeking
Frantically with his fingers.

RAINER MARIA RILKE:
REQUIEM FOR A WOMAN

This poem is a tribute to the painter Paula Modersohn-Becker, with whom Rilke carried on a platonic but emotionally intense relationship starting in 1900 and ending with her death in childbirth in 1907. In her lifetime Modersohn-Becker was known more as the wife of painter Otto Modersohn than as a painter in her own right. Today she is viewed as a major innovator in German Expressionist art, while her husband's work is regarded as competent and conventional.

The conflict between being her own person and being her husband's wife continued throughout Modersohn-Becker's career; she tried hard to be both at once. There were trips to Paris to soak up the latest art and trips to Berlin to attend cooking classes. At the end of her life she was preparing for the role of mother, a role she did not live to play.

Rilke, like many of Modersohn-Becker's associates, was slow to recognize the caliber of her talent. In this poem he renders an anguished and belated appreciation of the depth of her singular artistry.

I have my dead ones, and I let them go
And was amazed to see them so consoled,
So soon at home in being dead, so just,
Unlike their reputation. Only you
Return; you graze me, walking round, about
To bump something and make a sound of you,
Betraying you. Oh do not take from me
What I have learned so slowly. You are wrong
If anything at all can move you so
To homesickness. For we transform these things:
They are not here, but mirrored in to us
From out our being, as we catch sight of them.
    I thought you were much farther. It confuses me
That of all people, *you* should wander back,
Who transformed more than any other woman.
That we were frightened when you died, no, that
Your powerful dying darkly interrupted us,
Cutting the Formerly off from the Henceforth,
Is our concern, and to encompass that
Will be the work that we must do with everything.
But that you were afeared and even now
Harbor the fear, where fear is meaningless;
That you should lose a piece of your eternity;
That you should enter here again, friend, here,
Where nothing yet quite *is;* that you, confused,
In your first everything, confused and halfway,
Faced with the opening of the endless natures
Could fail to grasp them as you would grasp anything;
That from the circulation that received you,
The wordless sinker of some great unrest
Should pull you down again to counted time—
That wakes me like a burglar in the night.

If I could say you only deign to come
Out of the greatness of your heart's abundance,
Because you are so certain of yourself
That you walk round, a child not yet afraid
Of places where they'll do something to you—
But no: you plead. That is what chills my bones,
Pulling at them like sawteeth back and forth.
A grim reproach brought to me by your ghost,
Brought home to me at night, when I draw back
Into my lungs and into my intestines,
Into the last poor chamber of my heart,
Such a reproach would not be as macabre
As this, your pleading. What are you pleading for?

  Speak: should I travel? Is there anywhere
A thing you left behind that is tormented
And straining after you? Should I explore
A land you never saw, although it was
As close as your brain's other half to you?

  Then I will navigate its rivers, I
Will go on land and ask of ancient customs,
And I will speak with women in the doorways,
Observing how they call their children to them.
I'll notice how they take the landscape in
Around them as they go to the old work
Of fields and meadows; will desire that I
Be led into the presence of the king,
And will pay off the priests sufficiently
To set me down before the strongest icon
And go away and close the temple doors.
And finally, when I know these many things,
Then I will simply watch the animals,
That something of their movements may transpire

Into my joints; will have a short existence
There in their eyes, that hold me and then slowly
Let go, peaceably, without prejudice.
I then will cause the gardeners to recite
Long lists of flowers, so that in the shards
Of their fine Christian names I may bring back
Some trace of all their hundred fragrances.
And I will buy its fruits, its fruits that have
The land inside, as far up as the sky.

For that was your department: ripened fruits.
You used to put them in the pans before you
And weigh them out upon a scale of colors.
And as you saw the fruits, so you saw women,
And saw the children so, from inside out
Driven into the forms of their existence.
Finally you came to see yourself as fruit;
You peeled yourself of clothes and set yourself
Before the mirror, eased yourself on in,
All but your looking, which remained outside
And did not say *I am* but said *This is*.
So void of curiosity was your looking,
So stripped of gain, of such true poverty,
It no longer desired you even: holy.

I'd like to keep you where you used to put
Yourself: deep in the mirror, far away
From everything. Why do you come so differently?
Why do you contradict yourself? Why do
You try to make me think that in those beads
Of amber round your neck there was still gravity,
The kind of gravity that does not exist
In the beyond of peaceful images?
Why does your posture show me your misgiving?

What makes you lay your body's contours out
Like lines upon your palm, so that henceforth,
Seeing them, I must read your fate in them?
   Come in the candlelight. I do not fear
To look upon the dead. For when they come,
They have the right to stand there for a moment
Before our eyes, the same as other things.
   Come here: we will be still a little while.
Look at this rose upon my writing-desk:
Is not the light round it just as reluctant
As that round you? It should not be here either.
Out in the garden, unconfused with me,
It should have stayed or perished, but instead
It's here: what does it care about my consciousness?

   Don't be afraid if now I grasp, for oh,
I feel it rise in me, I cannot help it,
I have to grasp, and though it meant my death,
To grasp that you are here. There, I have grasped it.
Just as a blind man grasps something around him,
I feel your plight and know no name for it.
Come let us mourn together that someone
Pulled you out of your mirror. Can you cry still?
You can't. The strength and pressure of your tears
Is changed now to a riper looking-on.
You were about to channel all your sap
Into the currents of a stronger being
That rises up and flows, balanced and blind—
Had chance not pulled you back, ultimate chance
That pulled you from your farthermost advancement
Into a world again where the blood *wills*.
Not all at once; only a piece at first;

But as from day to day around this piece
The realness added on and made it heavy,
You needed all of you: and so you went
And broke yourself out of the law in pieces
Painstakingly, because you needed you.
Then you went down and dug out of your heart's
Nocturnal earth and warmth the still-green seeds
From which your death was meant to sprout: your own,
Your special death, the death of all your life,
And ate them then and there, your seeds of death,
Ate the death-seed like any other seed,
And had an aftertaste of sweetness in you,
All unintended, sweetness on the lips,
You: who were sweet already in your senses.
   Oh let us mourn. Do you know how your blood,
Caught up in a circulation like no other,
Reluctantly came back because you called it?
With what confusion it took up again
The body's smaller circulation, and
With what amazed distrust entered the womb,
Suddenly weary from the long way back.
You drove it on; you pushed it to the fore,
You dragged it toward the furnace, as one drags
A herd of victims to the sacrifice,
And asked it to be happy in the bargain.
And finally you compelled it: it came running
And gave itself up happily. You thought,
Being accustomed to the other measures,
That it was only for a while; except
Now you were back in time, and time is long.
And time goes on, and time adds up, and time
Is like the relapse of a chronic sickness.

How short your life was in comparison
With these long hours where you sat before
The many energies of your great future
And calmly bent them down to the new child-seed,
Which was a fate once more. Oh bitter labor,
Labor beyond all strength. And yet you did it.
Day after day you dragged yourself to work
And pulled the lovely weaving from the loom
And used your threads again a different way—
And finally put good face on your bad fortune.

   When it was done, you wanted your reward
Like children when they've drunk bittersweet tea
That hopefully will make them well again.
You found your own reward; you were too distant,
As always, from all others for another
To have imagined what reward would please you.
But you knew, and you sat up in your childbed.
And there before you was a looking-glass
That gave you back yourself completely. Now
That was all *you*, all *out there*, and inside
Only the sweet deceit of every woman
Who puts on jewels and combs and styles her hair.

   And so you died, as women used to die,
Old-fashioned dying in a cozy house,
The death of women in their childbearing
Who try to close themselves again and can't
Because the darkness that they also bore
Comes back again and forces its way in.

   But even so, shouldn't someone have hired
Some wailing-women? Women who weep for money,
And who, if you pay them right, will start a wail
At any hour of the night that grows too still.

More customs, please! We're running short on customs.
Everything goes and falls into disuse.
So you, the dead one, must come here to me
To get your mourning. Do you hear me mourn?
I wish my voice could be a cloth for you,
To drape across the fragments of your death;
I'd rip at it until it was in shreds,
And everything I say would have to go
Ragged and freezing in this voice—if just
Complaints were needed. But now I accuse:
Not the one man who pulled you out of yourself
(I cannot find him out; he's like the others),
But I accuse them all in him: the Man.

    If there should rise from deep within me somewhere
A child-that-has-been, something yet unknown,
Perhaps the purest childhood of my childhood,
I do not want to know of it. I'll take it
And shape it into an angel without looking,
And I will throw it into the first row
Of screaming angels that remind the Lord.

    For all this suffering has gone on too long.
No one can keep it up; it is too hard for us,
The crazy suffering of an unjust love,
That, building on seniority and habit,
Claims rights and lets injustice grow like weeds.
Where is the man who has the right to own?
And who can own what does not keep itself
But only sometimes makes a happy catch
And throws it back again like a child's ball.
As little as the captain can hold fast
To winged Victory figured on his bow
When, by the secret lightness of her godhead,

41

She is whisked off into the sparkling sea-wind:
So little can we call out to the woman
Who does not see us any more but walks
Miraculously, without accident,
On down the narrow strip of her existence—
Unless we have a taste for what is wrong.

   For that is wrong, if anything is wrong:
Not to increase the freedom of a loved one
By all the freedom that you find in you.
And everywhere we love, we have but this:
To let each other go; since holding on
Is easy, and we don't have to learn it first.

   Are you still there? What corner are you in?
You used to know so much of everything,
Could do so many things, as you walked out
Open to everything like breaking day.
Women suffer, true lovers are alone,
And artists at their labors sometimes sense
That everywhere they love, they must work change.
You started to do both; both are in that
Which fame distorts in taking it away.
But you were distant from all fame. You were
Inconspicuous, having softly taken
Your beauty in, as one takes down a pennant
On the gray morning of a working day.
You wanted nothing but a lifetime's work,
Which is undone for all that, still undone.
   If you are still there, if within this darkness
There still is any spot in which your spirit
Vibrates in sympathy with the shallow soundwaves
Which, lonely in the night, a single voice

Stirs up in the currents of a high-walled room,
Then hear me: help me. See, we are afloat,
Not knowing when we'll slide out of our progress
And into something we don't mean, in which
We get ourselves caught up as in a dream
And die in it and never do wake up.
No one is wiser. Anyone who puts
His blood into a lifelong work can find
One day he just can't keep holding it up there
And so its worthless poundage drags it down:
Because there is an ancient enmity,
Somewhere, between man's life and his great works.
That I may see it and may say it, help me.
    Come back no more. If you can bear it, be
Dead with the dead. The dead are occupied.
Help me so that it does not scatter you,
As things most distant often help: in me.

FOR A FRIEND
ON LATELY COMMENCING HIS LOVE LIFE

for John and Holly Bailey

Jumbled in body and in mind,
Slumped to your shoulders, extruding beyond the chair,
You sit obtusely.
          Love's such a simple blind;
A wonder that no one figures it out beforehand!
But this is your first time.

The cognoscenti among the passersby,
Remembering your long semesters and your caution,
Stop and applaud before they pass.
Long overdue, they mutter, long overdue;
But here at last. They speak at some length of her and you;
But none of them speak of love in abstract terms
Who have seen your big, slow heart, beating so strong.

FROM THE WINDOW

The sister siren up the street—
"Oh human children, what has happened now?"—
Fading from voicetop only to repeat,
It makes me wonder how

I could be brought to that impasse,
To yank the stopcocks on my tanks of fear,
Loosing in seven-colored clouds the gas
That lights on striking air.

You minstrelbird, you nightingale,
Injury, death, and sickness have removed
Your every holding-back; yours is a wail
That Greeks would have approved.

Could I be sent a grief so wide,
My voice would rise, irreparably unbound,
The future would fall away like a buildingside,
And men would jump from windows at the sound.

CHARLES BAUDELAIRE: MEDITATION

Be good now, O my Grief, and hold your grieving down.
You called for Evening, and already it descends,
And, in the thick obscurity that cloaks the town,
Brings peace to some, to others fear and troubled minds.

Now while the multitude of mortals with no name,
Whipped on by Pleasure, that relentless overseer,
Goes harvesting remorse in fertile fields of shame,
O my poor Grief, give me your hand, come over here,

Away. Look round the sky, how the departed Years
Lean over balconies in robes of yesteryear;
See from the deepest waves smiling Regret emerge;

See the old Sun asprawl beneath a tattered sky;
And, like a shroud trailing beyond the Eastern verge,
Oh hear, my sister, hear the gentle Night draw nigh.

SONG:
SONG FROM BAUDELAIRE

Hush now, my childish grief,
Sobbing and short of breath.
You called for evening,
And evening now is here.

And as it eases down
Over the anxious town,
Some find their peace there,
And others meet their fear.

Each, as he takes his rest,
Asks of his own regrets.
And when his question sleeps,
It blossoms on my lips.

All day the mass of men
Worked to increase their pain.
Leave them behind you.
My childish grief, come here.

Look round the darkning sky.
See how the years gone by,
In costumes old and grave,
They smile now, they smile now and they wave.

Hush now and listen well
Over the eastern hill,
With what soft footsteps
The night is drawing near.

BECAUSE I FEEL…

Because I feel
And cannot tell,
My heart is full,
Loving your soul
And keeping still

As bears a priest,
Close to his breast,
The Blessed Host,
The Sacred Guest,
The body of Christ,
The Eucharist.

RAINER MARIA RILKE:
PONT DU CARROUSEL

The sightless man upon the bridge who stands,
Gray like the boundarystone of nameless ranges,
He is perhaps the thing, that never changes,
Round which the mainspring of the heavens winds,
The distant planets' center of repose.
For all around him runs and bumps and goes.

He is the upright sentry at his station,
Set down in many paths perplexed and whorled,
The darkling entry to the underworld
Amidst a surface-loving generation.

GOING TO THE PRINTER'S:
A DIDACTIC POEM

for all the Helminskis

To measure the geography of paper,
You need small measures: a tad and a hair's-breadth.
The tad is a **pica**, six picas to the inch.
The hair's-breadth is a **point**, 72 points per inch.

Now then: the type-style, with dozens or hundreds of **fonts** to
choose from,
Some with serifs and some without.
Serifs? The hairline strokes that complete
The top and bottom of certain letters.
Look at a capital *I*, for instance:
One stroke or three?
Sans-serif type makes bolder headlines,
But serif type is more legible text.
Next:

How big are the letters? That's **point-size**, in points.
Look at some samples, see what looks right.

The space between lines, or **leading** (rhymes with "bedding")
Is not measured in half lines or lines.
It's any space you specify, measured in points
From one baseline to the next.
(Hint: if you're setting 12-point type,
You'll need at least 12 points space between lines.)

Finally, how wide a column do you need?
That's **line length** or **measure**, in picas and points.

If you take this poem to the printer,
I'd like it set preferably in Palatino,
Or else in Garamond or Baskerville,
In 10-point type, with 12-point linespacing,
In a column 30 picas, 6 points wide.*

---

*They went and set it in Garamond, in 11-point type with 13-point
line spacing, in a column only 24 picas wide.

PROOFREADERS*

When you're a proofreader, errors leap out at you,
Springing right off of the page.
Oh, how improvident! Oh, how conspicuous!
Oh, how too ghastly to gauge!

No, not *accomodate*! No, no, not *seperate*!
Spare me the worst: *supercede*.
Don't even mention the *grammer* and *calender*.
Leave me alone while I bleed.

When you're a proofreader, errors leap out at you:
Such is the proofreader's plight.
Please, when you're writing stuff, think of us proofreaders:
Try to get everything right.

---

* Proofreaders will note the nonstandard usage in this poem.

RAINER MARIA RILKE:
LOVESONG

How should I keep my soul in bounds, that it
May not graze against yours? How should I raise
It over you to other things above it?
Ah, if I only knew of someplace lost
That lies in darkness, I would gladly leave it
There in a strange and silent place, somewhere
Where all your depths may swing, and will not move it.
But all the things that touch us, me and you,
Take us together like a stroking bow
As from two strings it draws one voice along.
Upon what instrument have we been spanned?
And who the fiddler has us in his hand?
O sweet the song.

55th

So by the book you're fifty-five.
I think you look like porno live.

The massive axis of your shoulders
Draws gasps of fear from all beholders.
The hairy barrel of your chest
Renders your nudity well-dressed.
The ill intention in your eye
Makes love abide and virtue fly.

Too smooth of grip to bruise a grape,
Too strong for lions to escape,
Oh be you glad and be you merry,
My beautiful voluptuary.

TWO BIRTHDAY HAIKUS

I.

you've broken your own
record for consecutive
years of loveliness

II.

you come through the door
heart dances on its hind legs
like a dog for joy

HUGO VON HOFMANNSTHAL:
BALLAD OF OUTWARD LIFE

And children grow, they grow with eyes as deep
As ignorance, grow old and die forgotten;
And every man goes onward on his way.

And bitter fruits cling to the vine and sweeten,
And fall to earth by night like perished birds,
And lie upon the ground and spoil uneaten.

And still the wind is blowing, and again
We notice it, and make a deal of words,
And feel the pleasure in our limbs, and pain.

And roads run through the grass, and there are places,
One here, one there, with lamps and trees and rivers,
And dangerspots…and ghosts, with covered traces…

What purpose are they built for? these that never,
As many as they are, turn out the same,
While laughter, tears, and death change off forever.

What does it profit us? this children's game,
For us, the ever great and lonely ones,
Who roam but for the roaming, with no aim,

Nor count the points we round to head for home.
And still, how much is said when we say *Evening*,
A word from which deep thought and sadness runs

Like viscous honey from the hollow comb.

.

SONG:
LATER ON

And children born with deep brown eyes
Will soon grow overcast with words,
And fruit will sweeten on the vine
And fall by night like perished birds.

And winds will rise from oceanbeds,
And part the dust on prairie plains,
And pleat the snow where no one treads,
And slant the course of gentle rains.

And streets will run through grassy fields
Where lanterns swing and torches flare,
And some will creak with wagon-wheels,
And some will stand deserted there.

And learned men will send for books
To learn the pictures in the sky,
And guilty men will send for priests
To make their peace before they die.

DAYS TILL DEPARTURE

In the days remaining
        wings, ships, an overhead light and gone
In the days remaining
        edge from a color of sound
In the days remaining you walk through rooms
        fish, ships, and follow them through the sea.

Guitars and shadows will weave more tightly than calico thread and
                        thread
Strings of guitars will tangle lightly as golden hair
As hair on a golden head
        while white into gray, the gray sky.

In the days remaining you overhang me
        grass on the upland pasture brown
I watch your feet, that turn and are planted
        seed from the earth to the sower's hand
And thinking that even Love…
My hands would rise of themselves to shape you
Touch you
        only for fear
              and the light from eyes.

I can see the color of these days: it is brown through green.
The sounds are voices heard in the morning,
Asking each other if I have wakened.
The walls, these pale green walls, need help: they are shrinking.
The windows, that looked out, look back in and are frightened.
And thinking that even Love...
I would fasten you roughly, gauging my need
So closely
          fear
               and the lights and ships and sky.

RAINER MARIA RILKE:
THE GAZELLE

Enchanted creature, how can words aspire,
Though paired in tune, to learn the rhyming spells
That come and go in you like signal-bells?
From out your forehead rises leaf and lyre;

A likeness sends your qualities aloft
In songs of love, in which the lyrics, soft
As roseleaves, settle on the hand that puts
A volume down, and on the eye that shuts

To look at you: transported, so to speak,
As if the legs were charged with ammunition,
Kept back for now from springing while the neck
Holds up the head to hear—in such a fashion
As when the woodland bather halts in place,
The forest lake in her averted face.

RAINER MARIA RILKE:
THE PANTHER

His gaze, from the revolving bars that bound him,
Has grown so weary that it will not hold,
As if there were a thousand bars around him,
And then behind the thousand bars no world.

The supple steps, here hardened and here softened,
Turned round upon each other like a spring,
Suggest a dance of strength around a deafened
Will, fixed in the center of the ring.

At random points of time the pupil's valance
Goes softly up: A picture hits the eyes,
Goes through the members in their tightened silence,
And reaches to the heart and dies.

FREDERICK DOUGLASS: AN INVOCATION

Douglass, speak to us once more.
How urgently we need to hear
That voice, more like the ocean's roar
Or like a great cathedral choir
Than any now that reach our ear.

You shone the light of reason on
That which was palpably insane
To see what sense could be derived.
You simply did that to survive.
Your wrath was rich, your hatred nil.
You did that to survive as well.

Douglass, we really need you back.
We just don't seem to have much luck
At separating wrath from hate,
Being able to cooperate,
Or even able to coexist
Across the barbed wire of mistrust.

Also, our speakers are a bore,
A cloud of smog from ear to ear,
A glut of undifferentiated tongues
No Frederick Douglass is among.

Douglass, you must come back today.
Of course, you won't like what you see.
But please, we haven't got a clue.
In sheer despair we turn to you.
We too are palpably insane.
Tell us, what does *our* madness mean?
If not you, who can make it plain?

                              Douglass,

Speak to us again.

RAINER MARIA RILKE:
THE LONELINESS

The loneliness is like a rain.
It rises toward the evening from the main.
Up from the surfaces of distant plains
It gains the sky, its home. And only down
From out the sky it falls upon the town.

It drizzles downward in the halfway watches
When all the alleys turn and head for morning;
And when, no wiser for their one-night matches,
The bodies part, and set about returning;
And when the ones with hatred in them burning
Must share their bed, and cannot share their dreams:

Then loneliness down rivers and streams...

SONG:
LIKE A RAIN

The loneliness is like a rain
That rises skyward from the waters;
It gathers strength above the plain,
Then plunges down like gray marauders.
And the loneliness is like a rain,
And we must see what shelters still remain.

It batters down upon the hoods
Of cars confused by intersections;
It rises up in tiny floods
And spatters out in all directions.
And the loneliness is like a rain;
If someone walks too near, his clothes are stained.

It scatters in the doubtful light
When streets and alleys head for morning,
When bodies matched a single night
Draw back and set about returning.
And the loneliness is like a rain
That leaves a stigma on the windowpane.

At empty taverns and hotels
It knocks a while upon the shutters;
It rests in puddles where it fell,
Then gently brims into the gutters.
And the loneliness is like a rain,
Flowing down river out to sea again...

NUKE POEM

When I have fears that *we* may cease to be,
I think that I would gladly die.
Would?
I mean *will*, or will try to try.
But then, when Death shall eat me
And void me into black space utterly,
What will the difference be how green a world has disposed of me?
When the last singer of my songs
Has sold his guitar and no longer goes partying,
What do I care whether player and instrument
Are or are not to be holocaust-harvested?
There in the void, will I feel an additional layer of nothingness?

Why, in my dreams, so often and so soon—:
Undifferentiated dunes,
Contaminated dust,
Our history, the whole idea of us.

PAUL VERLAINE:
CLAIR DE LUNE

Your soul is an elaborate estate
Peopled with strolling harlequins and jesters
Plucking the lute and capering and yet
Somber somehow beneath their motley vestures.

For even as they chant in minor keys
Of love triumphant and life opportune,
Their own good fortune leaves them ill at ease,
Until their song is mingled with the moon,

Is mingled with the moonlight white and solemn
That brings a dream to birds on shady limbs
And puts a tremble in the water-columns,
The slender columns high above marble rims.

A TRIAL AUTOBIOGRAPHY

I.

Like others, he chopped his food into bits and burnt it,
Being as he was a fire,
And no sweet brushfire either,
But burning carrion of hogs and cattle.
His table manners were learned by observation from a dog.
What the secondhand stores couldn't sell, they gave to him
                                                    for clothes.

In the turbulence of his youth, he turned to homosexuality
                                                    and drugs.
It was to be a long collaboration.

Lord knows you were kind of in trouble if he *liked* you:
I mean, some found it sickening,
The way he hopped around you like an ingratiating rabbit;
Others were more pleased with the attention.
There was also one woman he particularly liked,
Who chose, for reasons of her own, to put up with him—
                                                    for a while.

II.

He took it philosophically enough
When he first found he had lost his power to shock,
But his calm soon turned to panic
When he beheld forgiveness closing in on him from all sides.
Still, he went on,
Bearing his adolescence high like a cross before him...

III.

He was good in the role of the old blind poet, toward the end,
Evoking pity and fear;
And he died, fortunately for our remembrance of him,
Before his hospital bills wore out his welcome.
When the last square inch of dirt had covered the last square inch
                                            of his coffin,
The mourners all joined hands,
And everyone heaved a sigh: "WHEW!
We'll miss him and all,
But at least NOW we can stop being polite about his so-called
                                            'writing.' "

RAINER MARIA RILKE:
THE FLAMINGOS

In mirror images like Fragonard's
Is nothing of their redness nor their whiteness
Beyond what could be given in a likeness,
Saying about a lovely girl: She was

Still soft with sleep. For if, amid the planting,
On coral stems adroitly pivoted,
They stand in clumps, like blossoms in a bed,
They court themselves with courtship more enchanting

Than Phryne's: till their necks reflex to harbor
Their pale eyes in their own sweet feather-arbor,
Where black and apple-red in hiding lies.

A sudden envy shrieks through the partition;
They, having stretched themselves in arch surprise,
Go stalking off into sheer supposition.

SLEEP IS RAINING DOWN FEATHERS…

Sleep is raining down feathers.
My fogbound head
joggles through minutes, muttering
What will the ship be? Where was the music?
Sometimes a madcap thought overplays its hand, and
I come to my senses.

Sleep barrages my head with bubbles
blown by familiar voices.
One floats close to my ear until
I can hear the words that are in it;
it spins in place like the earth
and pops—I'm alone.

Time to be off. At last there swim in my eyes
comforting bodies, known and imagined,
aroused with signs of surrender,
assuring me there's no evil done in dreams.

SONG: NIGHT-PIECE

Deep
under the leaves
a stripe of sound:
the moist cicadas.
Shades
break and rejoin
as lanterns stir
their lilyponds of light
and bells intone
the dead of night.

Birds
home from the air
lie couched in wood
and steeped in breathing.
Flowers
hark to the breeze
above their heads
and droop with heavy time
and speak of sleep
in pantomime.

YOU, TAKING SHAPE...

you, taking shape in my mind,
strange dalliance of weary nerves with the hope of the fallen,
patchwork of old-time tales and the present need

finding the roebuck or finding you,
at best I can station myself some place
where you might have reason to pass,
perhaps disguised, like a Shakespeare girl, as a man;
disguised, perhaps, as my own mirror image,
invisible at the last

I would like for a sign
to hang on the walls of public places:
your face, and the word Reward;
my pencil, poised to draw it, halts in my finger-ends

profuse maps, austere calendars
are silent of you; it is only sure
that on seeing you
I will call you by name, Necessity

CURRENTS OF THE HEART

They don't spark the gap.
They just fall flat.
They fall back.

Come have a look at them, poor hurt things
That wriggle and thunk as you look them over;
Look at them, stand with eyes of bronze,
And brood on your various powers.

Then, with a one-piece years-of-practice flick of the wrist,
Collect them, direct them,
Send them going through fingers and hands
Till the sense of touch no longer doubts them;
Send them around the house,
Send them through yards of wire;
And last, before you leave,

Transform them for me so that they will go
Relaxed and humming across the rest of the country,
Like wires that you see from the window of your car,
That seem to hum as you see them,
Simply because they rise and fall.

RAINER MARIA RILKE:
EVENING

The evening pauses for a change of vesture,
Which trees hold ready in their patient hands;
You watch, and see the lands in their departure,
A land ascending, and a falling land;

Which leave you there, in neither land quite resting,
Less darksome than the house benumbed in time,
Less able to conjure the everlasting
Than that which turns to star each night and climbs—

And leave to you, entangled and bizarre,
Your life, foreboding and immense and rising,
A thing that, now confined and now comprising,
Reverberates as stone in you and star.

THE MAD POETASTER

The sadness unseen, it is little and green,
But it riddles the ether with riddles obscene.
When it swells   brittle bells
Toll the saraband service of sadness unseen.

On the plaza I pace, and I ponder once more
The embarrassing odor of rot at the core.
And I feel myself bound for the dustful demesne
Of the cyclical sickness of sadness unseen.

                  —Which is little and green,
But it crunches its cud with a cunning unclean.
And it hits   and it spits
Out a sequence of sequins of sadness unseen.

The seraphim, even, have inwardly sinned,
Circling by ones in the westering wind.
Baptism balks; can I clutch for a screen
From the slithering slopes, from the rapid ravine?

The falling from faith where the scavenger skims,
The doubting of dawn when the daffodil dims—
My heart has lost harbor; I think it must lean
On the silicate scepter of—

Sadness unseen…it is little and green,
But it murmurs to meadows of aquamarine.
Let us whisper   let us whisper
The insistent encystment of sadness unseen.

HUGO VON HOFMANNSTHAL:
THE FOOL AND DEATH

Dramatis Personae:
DEATH
CLAUDIO, a nobleman
HIS SERVANT
THE DEAD:
   CLAUDIO'S MOTHER
   A LOVER OF CLAUDIO'S
   A FRIEND OF HIS YOUTH

Scene: Interior of Claudio's house
Time: Some centuries ago

(Claudio's study, in the Imperial style. Large windows in the background to right and left. In the middle a glass door leading out to a balcony, with a wooden staircase descending to the garden below. At left, a white folding door; at right, a doorway leading to the bedroom covered by a green velvet curtain. A desk stands by the left window with an armchair in front of it. Glass cases of antiquities stand by the pillars. Against the wall at right stands a dark carved Gothic chest, with antique musical instruments above it. There is a painting by an Italian master, nearly blackened by age. The color of the rug is light, almost white, with gold embroidery.)

CLAUDIO *alone*
(He sits by the window. Evening sun.)

The farthest mountains, as the sunlight changes,
    Are melted to a glaze of light and breath.
    Above them, with gray shadows and gold fringes,
Float clouds of marble in a perfect wreath.
So artists used to paint, in times foregone,
The clouds that the Madonna rode upon.

The cliffs are blue where clouds have cast their shadows;
The mountain's shadow falls on vale and stream
And mutes to gray the gleaming green of meadows;
The summit sparkles in a last full beam.
How close they are to all for which I yearn
Who till broad fields and seldom see their neighbor,
Whose handworked acres yield a rich return
On all the welcome weariness of labor.
It is the wonderful, wild morning breeze,
Hurtling barefoot through the fragrant heath,
Who wakens them; they live among wild bees
And draw the hot, clear air, which is God's breath.
Nature supplied their work and their resources;
It is in Nature that their wishes form;
The interplay of fresh and weary forces
Sustains them, makes them fortunate and warm.
The golden ball jerks downward now and sinks
Amid the far-off seas of crystal green;
The last light through the distant forest blinks;
Red smoke collects and breathes a glowing screen
That fills the strand till where the cities nestle
That reach with Næad arms from out the flood
And cradle their young in oceangoing vessels,
A race of men audacious, sly, and good.
They glide on distant, ponderous, and silent
Floods, that never a keel has cut in twain;
Their breast heaves with the anger of the violent
Sea, and they are healed of folly and pain.
Mercy and meaning thus I see extending
And gaze with longing at their distant shimmer;
But near and nearer as my sight is wending,
The scene grows empty, bitterer and dimmer.
It seems like all the life I've not been living,
Lost happiness, and unshed tears of mourning,

Around this house, around these alleys weaving
Eternal foolish quests, and senseless yearning.
(Standing at the window.)
They light their lamps and have within their narrow
Walls a close and heavy world, supplied
With gifts of drunkenness and sorrow
And all the rest that hearts can hold inside.
They live so closely, heart to heart,
And worry when it's time someone returned,
And when at times someone is hurt,
Console themselves…that's something that I never learned.
The simplest words and nothing more
Will tell their sorrows, joys, and angers;
They need not lunge at shuttered doors,
Or strike them with bloody fingers…

What do I know of human life?
It is a place where I have stood,
But only at best have understood,
Never been woven in its warp and woof,
Never been lost within the weave.
Where others took and others gave,
I sat in corners, stillborn and aloof.
I have not kissed the lips of love,
In the strong drink of life have never reveled,
And never down the street, pounding with pain,
Swallowing hard, no, never once have traveled.
And every time that I through Nature's gift
Have thought I felt a stirring or a lift,
I pounced upon it with my vigilant sense,
Which gave it a name and put it down to reasons.
Helpful comparisons streamed in by thousands;
The pleasure or the hope itself was hence.

And even pain!—diminished and depressed
With thinking, nondescript and undistinguished!
I meant to hold it fiercely to my breast;
I would have wrestled ecstasy from anguish:
Its wings but grazed my shoulder; I was spent.
And so discomfort came, and anguish went...
(Coming to himself.)
...Well, well, so time flows on. It's getting late.
What sense is there to stand and ruminate?
I'm tired now and I think I'll go to bed.
I see now, by the light my lantern sheds,
The rubble and the relics kept in store,
Through which I knocked around with footsteps creaking,
But never found the straight path or broad door
That gave upon the life that I was seeking.
(In front of the crucifix.)
Beneath this wounded ivory, your feet,
Christ crucified, have many sought direction,
Calling for mercy to the Paraclete
To send the flames that move the heart to action.
And when not fire but void and coldness came,
They fell into confusion, fear, and shame.
(In front of an old picture.)
Gioconda, with your wondrous background, lit
With the soft lighting of transfigured limbs,
The mouth imponderable and sweet,
The eyelids heavy with their dreams,
You showed me just as much of life unmasked
As I ascribed to you in questions asked.
(Turning aside, in front of a cabinet.)
You crystal cups, at whose cool rim have hung
So many lips in sweet dumbfounding,
You lutes of old, you at whose sounding
So many hearts in deep accord have rung,

80

What I would give to be besieged by wonder,
With what humility I would surrender!
You works in iron and in bronze,
You pictures, sprung from baffling fonts
Of turtles, angels, griffins, trolls,
Frightening and intoxicating things,
Fantastic birds and golden scrolls,
But all conceived in man's imaginings,
And born from twitching, living moods,
Thrown up by the great oceanfloods,
And now caught fast in form, as fishes in the seine!
I have gone after you in vain;
Your charm has tied me all too closely to you.
And when I'd held up your eccentric souls
Like masks in turn, and stood there looking through you,
My life, my heart, my world to me were veiled;
You held me, like a fluttering swarm, assailed
And bit, like the Harpies that were Phineus' doom,
From every living stem the living bloom.
I lost myself so much in art and craft
I could not see the sun but with dead eyes;
My ears were dead, I had no hearing left:
I dragged with me the enigmatic curse,
Never quite known and never quite unknown,
With sorrows petty, pleasures monotone,
Living my life out like a book of verse,
One half not yet, one half no longer understood,
That keeps the sense from seeking out its livelihood;
In joy or sorrow, it did not occur
To me that these meant simply what they were:
They had to be the glimmerings of the future
Or premonitions of a fuller nature.

And so in all my labors and my loves,
Confused with shadows, I have fumbled on,
Consumed, but had no pleasure from, my drives,
In the dull dream that it would finally dawn.
I turned around and looked Life in the face:
In which the race is never to the swift,
The battle never to the brave; in which
Misfortune gives no pain, nor Fortune joy,
Where questions void of sense meet senseless answers,
Where jumbled dreams rise dimly from black caves,
And luck is all: the hour, the wind, the waves!
My wisdom's pain, my disappointment's gall
Are wrapped in weary pride, and by abstaining
I live in my cocoon without complaining,
In this small town, within this narrow wall.
The people of the place have stopped explaining;
They find me not unusual at all.
(The Servant comes and puts a plate of cherries on the table, then goes to close the balcony doors.)
Leave the doors open—what on earth is frightening you?

SERVANT

Your Grace will probably not believe me.
(To himself, anxiously.)
And now they're hiding in the summer-house.

CLAUDIO

Who?

SERVANT

Your pardon, but I just don't know.
A great unholy swarm of ghostly wanderers.

CLAUDIO

Beggars?

SERVANT

I just don't know.

CLAUDIO
          Then shut the door
That leads into the garden from the streets
And go to bed and lie between the sheets.
          SERVANT
But that's exactly what unnerves me. I
Did shut the garden door and locked it.
          CLAUDIO
                                        Well?
          SERVANT
They're sitting in the garden. On the bench
Where the sandstone Apollo stands, a pair
In shadows off beside the fountain's rim,
And one has seated himself upon the Sphinx.
The Taxus is in the way, so you can't see him.
          CLAUDIO
Are they all men?
          SERVANT
          No, some of them are women.
Not beggarly, but dressed in bygone styles;
They have on clothes like those in old engravings.
What's more, they have a horrifying way
Of sitting still and looking with dead eyes;
They look at you as if at empty air.
Those are no human beings. Please Your Grace
Not to be angry, but I would not want
To let them near me, not for anything.
Please God, they will be gone tomorrow morning.
For now—with your permission—I will lock
The doorway from the house up tight and sprinkle
The castle halls with holy water. For
Those are no people such as I have seen
And people do not look with eyes like theirs.

CLAUDIO

Do as you wish, and so good night.
(He walks a while back and forth, lost in thought. Offstage the melancholy and compelling sound of a violin is heard, distant at first, gradually nearing, finally warm and full, as if issuing from a neighboring room.)

Music?
And speaking strangely to the very soul!
Is this my servant's madness, or my own?
I feel as if I'd never heard
From earthly fiddles such a tone…
(Pauses to listen, turned toward the right side.)
It bears a deep and longed-for thrilling
And surges over me within.
It seems like infinite fulfilling;
It seems like limitless chagrin,
As if my life was changed with light and spilling
From ancient walls and streaming in.
Like the return of mother or beloved,
Of all that I have waited long to see,
It rouses holy thoughts, still warm and vivid,
And flings me out upon a childhood sea.
One distant spring I stood atop a summit
And thought I would float into the One-and-All,
With boundless yearning over every limit
And premonitions round me like a squall.
And there were journeys where my spirit circled
Until the whole world shone at once, and bells
Sang out their notes to me, and roses sparkled,
Rejoicing in a light from somewhere else.
How much of life there was in every creature;
How they came forward to my loving touch;
What awe I felt, what gladness to be such
A living member in the chain of nature!

And I could feel, just as my own heart led me,
The stream of Love that nourishes all hearts,
With fullness that took hold of me and spread me,
Which now not even my fondest dream imparts.
Play onwards, music, do not end your song
Until your notes have reached my inmost cell;
And I shall think my life is glad and young,
And live it backwards underneath your spell:
For all the flames I love, with tongue on tongue,
Are melting the ice, making the waters swell!
The dreariness and datedness of learning,
This burden that has lain upon my bones,
Now hears the primitive consciousness returning,
And vanishes in deep and child-like tones.
Far off, with many sounds of bells,
I hear proclaimed a yet-undreamed-of living,
Whose forms mean more than anyone can tell,
Powerful and clear in taking and in giving.
Listen! It vanishes as it began,
In which I heard the notes of god and man!
And he who sent this wonderworld within
Has doubtless raised his hat to catch a coin or two,
A gypsy wanderer with a violin.
(At the window on the right.)
He's not down there. That doesn't seem quite right!
Where then? I'll try this other window here…
*(As he moves toward the door at right, the curtain is softly drawn
back, revealing Death standing in the doorway, with his violin hang-
ing from his belt and the bow in his hand. He looks calmly at
Claudio, who recoils in horror.)*
Why do I feel this senseless, nameless fear?
Why, if your fiddle's sound was such delight,
Why does it so constrict my throat to see you,
And bristles the hair and draws the heartstrings tight?

Get out! Get out! Death! What are you doing here?
I am afraid. Go! I can't even shout,
I'm losing hold of things, I'm losing air!
Who called you? Who admitted you? Get out!
                DEATH
Stand up! Leave off this whimpering and shudders.
I'm not a bogeyman, I'm not a troll;
I am a great god of the human soul,
And Eros and Dionysus are my brothers.
When in the moistness of a summer evening
Through golden air a leaf floats down and clings,
My breeze it is that makes you shiver,
That weaves around the ripenesses of things.
When overtopping swells of feeling
Flooded your soul with warmth until it trembled,
When Dread ripped off her veil, so that you saw
That it was you whom she the most resembled,
When you surrendered, when you found
The world was yours, and danced in the great round,
In every truly noble hour
That shivered through your form and took control,
It was my sacred and mysterious power
That reached to the foundation of your soul.
                CLAUDIO
Enough! I welcome you, despite my fear.
(Pause.)
But aren't you going to say…what brings you here?
                DEATH
My business, friend, is *always* the same one.
                CLAUDIO
But not with me; it can't be! I'm not done!
Before the leaf can wither, it has thrived;
The juices ooze away, but first they gather.
Too much is missing still: I haven't lived!

86

DEATH
You've gone along your way like every other!
                CLAUDIO
As thin, uprooted meadowflowers
Are swept along by a dark eddy,
So glided forth all my young hours;
I never knew I was alive already.
I stood before life's iron portals,
Afraid of wonders, driven with the restless heart,
Hoping that even for the least of mortals,
The thundering wings would fly apart.
It never came—and then, all of a sudden,
I stood inside, of holiness bereft,
With me and all my deepest wishes hidden,
Encumbered with a spell that never left.
Confused with dawn and dusk, hollow and huddled,
Disheartened in my inwardness and muddled,
My heart in two, my senses half denied me,
Forever short of fullness, strangely pent,
I felt no warmth that was a warmth inside me,
Nor any wave that took me where it went.
I never met the God in desert places
With whom one wrestles, and obtains his graces.
                DEATH
What each received, to you as well was given:
An earthly life, and earthly means of living.
In each of you a spirit springs
That breathes a unifying thought
Into this chaos of dead things,
To make yourself a garden-plot
For industry, for sorrow, and for bliss:
And woe to you, if *I* must tell you this!
Sometimes held and sometimes holding,
Through vague and violent hours to your unfolding;

87

Crying yourself to sleep, wearied with care,
Still heavy with desire, close to despair,
Deepbreathing with the urge of life, still warm,
But always *ripe*, you fall into my arm.

CLAUDIO

But I am unripe, therefore let me be.
I promise never to malinger,
But grasp the earth with every reverent finger;
The deepest lust for life cries out in me.
Fear knocks at my old curses, and they give;
I feel now—let me be—that I can live.
I feel a boundless urge in me that sings
That I can hang my heart on earthly things.
Henceforward I shall look at people squarely,
And not as animals or a puppet show.
All that is theirs shall touch my heart so nearly
That I have access to their joy and woe.
I will learn loyalty, the only hold
We have on life. I'll act in such a way
That good and evil always have control
Of me and always make me wild and gay.
My phantoms will turn human, and start living.
I will find people on the roads I've passed,
No longer mute in taking and in giving,
Be bound by them—oh yes—and bind them fast.
(Noticing Death's unchanged expression, with mounting anxiety:)
But don't you see, that was not so before:
What? Do you think that I have loved and loathed,
That I have seen the core of things unclothed?
I have seen words and semblances, no more.
Look here, and I can show you: letters, see,
(He yanks open a drawer and takes out a packet of old letters.)

Oaths, tears, and all the trappings of romances;
But do you think I ever *felt* as she,
Or *felt* the words I wrote in my responses?
(He throws the packet at Death's feet, so that the individual
letters fly out.)
Right there you have the whole romantic story,
Where only I and I called and resounded,
Rising or falling, as the mood would vary,
Till every sacredness was left confounded.
There! There! And the rest of it is all the same:
No sense, no love, no hate, no joy, no pain!

DEATH

You fool, you abysmal fool, I mean for you
To honor life just once before you're through.
Now stand against the wall there and keep still,
And learn that all the rest on earth's expanses
Were filled with worldly love and earthly senses,
And only you are fatuous and nil.
(Death plays a few phrases on his violin, as if calling. He stands by
the bedroom door downstage right, while Claudio stands against the
wall at left. Enter Claudio's Mother by the door at right. She is not
very old. She wears a long black velvet gown, a black velvet hood with
a white ruffle that frames her face. In her delicate, pale fingers is a
white lace handkerchief. She steps softly through the door and walks
soundlessly through the room.)

MOTHER

How many old, sweet pains I breathe again
Mixed with the air. As if from sprigs of lavender
A delicate dead current breathes a half
Of what I was on earth around me here:
A mother's life: one third of it is pain,
One worry, and one sorrow. What do men
Know about that? The edge, is it still sharp there?
He hit his head there once and bloodied his temple.

89

That's how he was, small, violent, wild when
He ran. I couldn't hold him. There, the window!
That's where I stood and listened late at night,
Listening for his steps with such a yearning
When worry wouldn't let me keep in bed,
When he didn't come, and it struck two, and then
Struck three and even started to get light out…
How often…yet he never knew a thing…
Of course I was alone by daylight too.
The hand has flowers to water, dust to beat
From cushions, knobs and lamps to rub and shine.
So runs the day. Only the head has nothing
To do. So it goes round in a dull wheel
Of premonitions, overcast with dreams
And loaded down with pain and secrets, which
I'm certain has something to do with what
I cannot say, with motherhood, with what
Is secret, what is holy, and the fabric
Of this, the world. But it is not my lot
To stay here with the sweet oppressive air,
The painful nourishing air. I cannot breathe.
I must be going, going…
(She exits by the middle door.)

                    CLAUDIO
                              Mother!
                    DEATH
                                        Silence.
You will not bring her back.
                    CLAUDIO
                              Ah, Mother, come!
And let me press my lips to yours once more,
These trembling lips, that always were too mute,
Too proud, too narrow; let me sink before
You on my knees and… Call her! Hold her still!

She didn't want to! Don't you see?! You brute,
Are you going to make her go against her will?
                    DEATH
Leave me what's mine. It *was* yours.
                    CLAUDIO
                              Ah, and never
Felt! Dry, all of it dry! When have I ever
Perceived how all the roots of what I was
Surged tremblingly toward her, and that her presence
Was meant, like presences of gods, to thrill
Me through with wonder and instill
A human yearning, human pain and pleasance?
(Death, unmoved by his complaints, plays the tune of an old folksong.
A young girl enters slowly, wearing a simple dress in a floral print,
cross-band shoes, and a bit of a veil around the neck; her head is
bare.)
                    THE GIRL
It was so sweet… You haven't forgotten, have you?
Of course it turned out sadly, dear, so sadly…
But what do we do that doesn't end in pain?
I've seen so few days that were ever happy,
But those few were as sweet as I could know.
The flowers in the window-box, my flowers,
The wobbly little spinet, the old cupboard
In which I put your letters and the gifts
That now and then you gave me…all those things—
Please don't make fun of me—those things were beautiful,
And each of them had something sweet to say.
When after a heavy evening the rain came
And we stood at the window…ah, the smell
Of dripping trees… And all of that is gone,
And all that was alive in it is buried
Inside the tiny coffin of our love.
But still, it was so sweet, and you're to blame
That it was sweet. To think that later on

91

You threw me over, heedless, as a child
Gets tired of his game and drops his flowers and leaves them…
My God, I had no hold on you at all.
(Brief pause.)
And then when your last letter came, the bad one,
I wished to die—I don't want to torment you
By saying that. I meant to write a letter
By way of taking leave: without complaint,
Not violent, with no great bursts of sorrow;
I only meant that maybe once again
You might be homesick for my love and me
And cry a bit because it was too late.
I never wrote the letter. No… Why should I?
How could I know how much of your real heart
Was in the things that filled my silly mind
With shining lights and fever, till at last
I walked in a dream by the broad light of day.
Good will will never change bad faith to good,
And tears will make no dead thing come alive.
It doesn't kill you, either. Only later,
After a long and miserable time,
I got to die. And in my last request,
I asked to be with you in your dying hour.
Not cruelly, and not to punish you,
But like when someone drinks a cup of wine
And unexpectedly the smell reminds him
Of something sweet: dim, forgotten, and somewhere.
(She exits. Claudio buries his face in his hands. As soon as she leaves, a Man enters of about Claudio's age. He wears a disheveled, dusty traveling costume. The wooden handle of a knife protrudes from his chest on the left. He comes to a halt in the middle of the stage, facing Claudio.)

THE MAN

And are you living still, eternal gambler?
Still reading Horace and delighting in
His mocking, clever, unimpassioned mind?
With delicate phrases you drew close to me,
Seemingly gripped by that which moved me also…:
I put you, so you said, in mind of things
That stilly slept within you, as the night-
Wind talks at times of its far destination…
Oh yes, you were a fine harp in the wind,
And the infatuated wind to play you
Each time was someone else's wasted breath,
No matter mine or whose. I guess that we were
Friends a long time. For after all, we shared
Our talk at every hour of day and night,
Dealings with like acquaintances, and even
Affairs with the same woman. Yes, we shared them
In much the way that slave and master share
House and sedan, dog and table and horsewhip:
The house is one's delight, the other's prison;
One rides in the sedan, the other's shoulder
Is red with its carvings; one says "Whup!" and the dog
Springs through a hoop, the other feeds and walks him…
The cloudy, halfdone feelings, my soul's pearls,
Painfully born, you took away and played
At catch with them like a new plaything—you,
Who made friends quickly, dealt with them so readily,
I with a mute appeal locked in my soul
And teeth clenched shut; and you without reserve
Fingering everything, while all my words
Died of mistrust or shyness on the way.
But then a woman came our way. And what
Took me, as sicknesses come over one
Where all the senses tumble, overwakeful

93

From too much gazing on a distant goal—
On such a goal, full of sweet melancholy
And wild light and aroma, from deep blackness
Shooting like thunder and lightning—all of that
You saw, it fascinated you! "Because
I'm much the same myself at certain times,
The girl's tired manner fascinated me,
Her bitter pride, her sense of disappointment
At such an early age." That's what you wrote
Me afterwards. It fascinated you!
To me it was more than this blood and brain!
And having played your fill, you threw the puppet
To me, with all her image nauseated
From you, so horribly wrenched and distorted,
So stripped of the enchantment and the wonder,
The features senseless, and the living hair
Scraggly and dead—you handed me her death-mask,
First having putrefied with vicious skill
The enigmatic sweetness and the charm.
For this at last I finally grew to hate you
The way my dark foreboding always hated you
And shunned your face. My destiny then drove me,
Granting at last to my fragmented person
One goal and one intention in my spirit—
My spirit, which despite your poisonous presence
Was not quite dead to all desires forever—
Ah yes, my lofty destiny then drove me
To fall to death upon this murderous blade,
Then threw me in a ditch beside an alley,
In which I lay and slowly decomposed
For things that you will never understand.
Yet three times blest compared to you, to whom
No one was anything, nor you to them.
(Exits.)

CLAUDIO

No, nothing to anyone, nor they to me.
(Slowly getting up.)
Like on the stage a bad comedian,
He comes on cue and speaks his part and goes,
Indifferent to the rest of it and bland,
Quite unaffected by the way he sounds,
Quite ineffective to the few who hear him:
So I for my part over the human stage
Have lumbered and lurched to no effect at all.
Why did that happen? Why must you, O Death,
Be he who makes me see life eye to eye,
No longer through a veil, but live and whole,
Awaking me at last, and passing by?
Why is the childish sense so overtaken
With high presentiments of earthly things
That then the things, when they come true, can waken
But shallow thrills and vague rememberings?
Why does the music of your violin
Not drive to light the hidden spirit worlds
That every breast in secret holds,
That now lie choked, by consciousness unspoken,
As flowers in debris lie soiled and broken?
Why can't I be with you, hear nothing else,
Not hampered with the petty and the false.
Why not? Your threats shall be a boon instead:
And Death shall be my life! since all my life was dead.
What forces me, who know nothing of either,
To call the nearer life, and death the farther?
You have the might to concentrate more living
Than lifetimes could contain into an hour.
I will put by the vague and the deceiving
And worship at your miracles and power.

Perhaps these are a dying man's pretenses
Driven up by frantic and expiring blood,
But I have never yet with all my senses
Perceived so much, and so I call it good.
And if the hour should end, and I expire,
But with my brain so full and so entire,
Then farewell, shallow life, farewell again!
Only now that I die, have I ever been.
When someone dreams, sometimes an overflow
Of dreamt emotion brings the dream to breaking;
And I awake, through such an overflow,
From Life's enchantment into Death's awaking.
(He falls dead at Death's feet.)
                    DEATH
(Exits slowly, shaking his head.)
How strange and wonderful these creatures—
To read what never yet was written,
To draw what has no face nor features,
Things unbondable to bind,
And pathways in the eternal dark to find.
(He disappears through the middle door as his words reverberate. It is still in the room. Through the window outside, the figure of Death passes playing his violin, followed by the Mother, the Girl, and a figure resembling Claudio.)
                    CURTAIN

FOOD SHORTAGES

Consider the food shortage. What is a food shortage?
The world can produce its food, and we have vehicles.
So there can't be a food shortage, only an organization shortage,
Or a cooperation shortage, with tariffs and frontiers,
Plus a language barrier, plus an education gap.
In short, these food shortages of which we continue to speak,
        because people die of them,
Are ulceratingly real and wholly a mental creation:
The infant gnawing on garbage bones
Has failed to make a dent in a heart in corporate Michigan;
And those that die thirsty and unwashed
Needed the revivifying rain that never fell
On some poor Washington DC cerebrum.

THE EPITAPH OF ÆSCHYLUS

Æschylus son of Euphorion lies here, a true son of Athens.
Sicily's flame-gold wheat
                    circles his grave with its fire.
Go ask the plains of Marathon what kind of courage he
                                showed there.
Go ask the long-haired Mede:
                    he would remember the name.

LEONIDAS TARANTINOU:
THE TOMBSTONE OF TELLEN

I am the tombstone of Tellen, the old man is buried beneath me.
He used to write funny songs

                              back when nobody knew how.

LINES WITH FOUR FEET

The day goes blah, the day becalms;
The hands on the clockface twiddle their thumbs;
The chair and the footstool sit on their hams;
But then—an end of a string unwinds
And dangles down my mind.
Catthoughts paw at the string and miss
Three times on purpose before they hook:
Skirdily, skirdily, skirdily, chook!
But big-dog thoughts with four feet flush
Leap at the cats and yap and spit.
Rowr-rowf!   Ss-st!
No one around to break it up,
And there would never be peace except
That thoughts of you, like pandabears,
Come padding in. Hi, bears.

THE WORLD PASSES FROM UNDER OUR FEET...

the world passes from under our feet helminski
by the time we're thirty-two we'll have disappeared
but I've got our next life all planned out
we'll be on bali playing in the same gamelan
I'll be furious with you because you'll make so many mistakes
but the hash will be good, and the shy and sun-bronzed
                                        island girls
will burn for you like hibiscus

RESPONSE TO A CRITIC OF MY SONGWRITING

The rhymes that I use
Are the ones that I choose,
Often funky and quite unconventional.
You may think they sound good,
You may think they sound bad,
But the sound that they make is intentional.

A FEW THINGS STRAIGHT

The love of men for men is hot and strong:
 It won't be satisfied for long.
The love of men for men is seen in public places
 Where gay guys show their frisky faces.
The love of men for men is friendly and warm:
 A hearth during a thunderstorm.
The love of men for men is from the heart:
 Sometimes it rips a guy apart.
The love of men for men is from the soul:
 Men who love men need men to make them whole.
The love of men for men will never die:
 You cannot kill us if you try.

RAINER MARIA RILKE:
THE LAST SUPPER

They sit assembled, credulous and furtive,
With him who like a sage is closed in thought,
Who takes himself from these whom he was part of,
And flows beyond their heads, and knows them not.
He feels the coming-on of loneliness,
In which his deep necessity was nourished;
Now he will wander in the olive forest;
Who love him most, will flee him in distress.

He asked to eat with them before he leaves;
And, as a bullet scatters birds from sheaves
Of grain, he scatters their fingers from the loaves
With this, his word. They crumple at his knee;
They flutter vaguely through the hall, intending
To find a window or a door. But he
Is all around them, like the dusk descending.

WILHELM BUSCH:
THE FOX AND THE FARMER

The fox was breathing the forest air.
The farmer sent him a letter there.
"Please do come by! All is forgiven;
There is no need for getting even.
The cock, the hens and all the geese
Will greet you with the kiss of peace.
And so: when should we have the party?
　　　　　Yours in true friendship,
　　　　　Christian Hardy"
The fox wrote back in goose's blood:
"Doesn't look good:
My wife just had another brood!
I send, as always, my highest regard.
　　　　　Your friend in the cave,
　　　　　Renard"

SONATA IN R

This morning I tried to open the door.
The results were poor.
You see, I wasn't quite sure
Which of the three keys there were
Went with which door.
Perhaps, if I'd been,
I'd have gotten in.
But as things were,
I stood and tried the key in the door,
And it went in the lock, but no more.
It didn't respond to the oaths I swore!
But that was the key, I was almost sure.

Almost…but no, not certain quite,
And so, by the ill-placed windowlight,
I looked through all of the keys I had,
Like a man gone mad,
Telling with my two eyes the story
Of each incursion and promontory,
Until, beyond the shadow of a gnat,
I'd distinguished this one apart from that.
In fact, the key I had was right.

This time, first time I tried,
The door opened wide.
Why didn't it do that the time before?
Stupid door!
It's weird: almost as if the key
Needed something from me.
Well yes, I guess the answer's there:
That *is* how things are.
Once you don't doubt the key any more,
Once you're sure,
It opens the door.

WILHELM BUSCH:
THE HUMORIST

Stuck fast in birdlime on his tree,
The bird flaps hard, but can't get free.
A big black cat comes creeping low;
His claws are sharp, his eyes aglow.
On up the tree and ever higher,
The murderous beast approaches nigher.
The bird thinks: "Well, since that is that—
I must be eaten by the cat—
I will not let a moment go,
I'll practice all the trills I know
And whistle merrily, undeterred."
I call that humor in a bird.

RAINER MARIA RILKE:
SONNET TO ORPHEUS #9

Only who sat among shades
Sounding the zither
Will find that the infinite praise
Is his to deliver.

Only who ate with the dead
Of the poppies they brought him
Will never release from his head
The tones that they taught him.

And oft though the face in the pond
Moves and is sundered,
Remember the form.
Not till the land of two lands
Shall voices be rendered
Deathless and warm.

www.ingramcontent.com/pod-product-compliance
Lightning Source LLC
Chambersburg PA
CBHW031325040426
42443CB00005B/212